This journal belongs to

Carrie Parker

Ancient Secrets of Essential Oils-the Journey
Beverly Banks

First edition

Holy Moly Media Company
5002 Herndon Circle
Colorado Springs, CO 80920
Visit our website at EssentialOilMovie.com

Graphic design by Bonnie McDermid, Wordsmith Ink

ISBN: 978-0-9977032-0-7

Printed in the United States of America

Table of Contents

Aloes or Sandalwood

Daily Uses
Sandalwood is used in ultra-hydrating moisture creams. Simply massage gently onto face, neck and other desired areas. Use daily after cleansing and toning your face.

Biblical References
He was accompanied by Nicodemus, the man who earlier had visited Jesus at night. Nicodemus brought a mixture of myrrh and aloes, about seventy-five pounds.

John 19:39

More References
Numbers 24:6
Psalms 45:8
Proverbs 7:17

When I experience Aloes/Sandalwood...

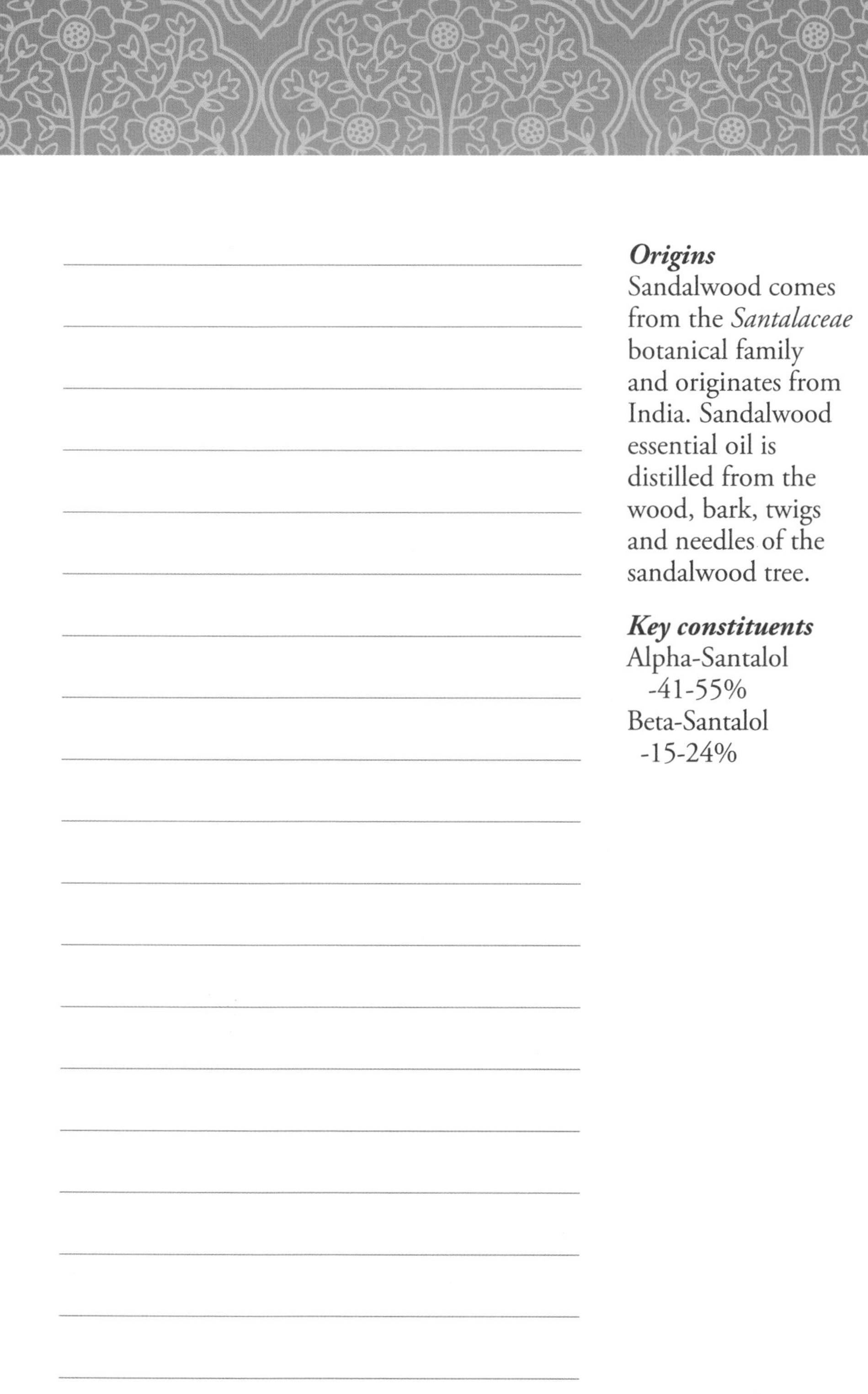

Origins
Sandalwood comes from the *Santalaceae* botanical family and originates from India. Sandalwood essential oil is distilled from the wood, bark, twigs and needles of the sandalwood tree.

Key constituents
Alpha-Santalol
-41-55%
Beta-Santalol
-15-24%

Aloes or Sandalwood

When I experience Aloes/Sandalwood...

Biblical aloes, also known as Sandalwood, has been known for its ability to nuture various body systems.

Calamus

Daily Uses
Soothing effect on tired muscles. Supports healthy respiratory and digestive systems.

Biblical References
Take the following fine spices: 500 shekels of liquid myrrh, half as much (that is, 250 shekels) of fragrant cinnamon, 250 shekels of fragrant calamus,

Exodus 30:23

More References
Ezekiel 27:19
Song of Songs 4:13-14

When I experience Calamus...

Origins
Acorus calamus is from the botanical family *Araceae*. The essential oil is distilled from the stems and leaves.

Key constituents
Ketones-40%
Phenols-30%
Aldehydes-7%

Interesting Fact
In ancient times, Calamus was used in the holy anointing oil, perfumes and incense.

Calamus

When I experience Calamus...

Cassia

Daily Uses
Supports the immune system and builds the body's natural defenses. Diffuse, apply topically, take orally or use as incense.

Biblical References
All your robes are fragrant with myrrh and aloes and cassia; from palaces adorned with ivory, the music of the strings makes you glad.

Psalms 45:8

More References
Exodus 30:24
Ezekiel 27:19
Job 42:14

When I experience Cassia...

Origins
Cinnamomum cassia is from the botanical family *Lauraceae* and originates from China.
The essential oil is steam distilled from the branches, leaves and petioles.

Key constituents
Cinnamic aldehydes-80%
Phenols-8%
Coumarins-7%
Esters 5%

Interesting Facts
Cassia is rich in Biblical history and is mentioned in the Ebers Papyrus, one of the oldest medical books, dating from the 16th century B.C.

While its aroma is similar to cinnamon, Cassia is chemically and physically quite different.

Cassia

When I experience Cassia...

Cassia nourishes the body and spirit by stimulating feelings of joy, happiness and emotional healing.

Cedarwood

Daily Uses
Supports deep sleep and promotes mental clarity.

Biblical References
The priest is to put some of the oil remaining in his palm on the lobe of the right ear of the one to be cleansed, on the thumb of their right hand and on the big toe of their right foot, on top of the blood of the guilt offering.
Leviticus 14:17

More References
Leviticus 14: 4, 6, 49

When I experience Cedarwood...

Origins
Cedrus atlantica is from the botanical family *Pinaceae* and originates in Morocco and the U.S.A. Cedarwood is the species most closely related to the Biblical cedars of Lebanon. The essential oil is steam distilled from the tree's bark.

Key constituents
Cedarwood is the essential oil known to be the highest in sesquitepenes–98%.
Sesquiterpene
- hydrocarbons-58%
- alcohols-22%
- ketones-18%

Interesting Fact
King Solomon built his palace and temple from cedarwood, which allowed him to continually breathe the cedarwood oil, enhancing his ability to think clearly and make wise decisions.

Cedarwood

When I experience Cedarwood...

Cinnamon

Daily Uses
Supports healthy cardiovascular and digestive systems. May support healthy blood sugar balance.

Biblical References
I have perfumed my bed with myrrh, aloes and cinnamon
Proverbs 7:17

More References
Exodus 30:23
Song of Songs 4:14
Revelation 18:13

When I experience Cinnamon...

Origins
Cinnamomum verum is from the botanical family *Lauraceae* (laurel). The essential oil is steamed distilled from the bark.

Key constituents
Aldehydes-47%
Phenols-25%
Sesquiterpenes-6%

Interesting Fact
Listed in Dioscorides' *De Materia Medica*, Europe's first authoritative medical guide which dates from A.D. 78.

Cinnamon

When I experience Cinnamon...

Cypress

Daily Uses
Supportive of the cardiovascular system and the female reproductive system. Promotes feelings of security, grounding. Cypress promotes production of leucocytes, which support the body's immune system.

Biblical References
I will put in the desert the cedar and the acacia, the myrtle and the olive.
I will set junipers in the wasteland, the fir and the cypress together,

Isaiah 41:19

More References
Isaiah 44:14

When I experience Cypress...

Origins

Cypress (*Cupressus sempervirens*) comes from the botanical family known as *Cupressaceae* and originates from Spain. Its essential oil is extracted by steam distillation of the branches.

Key constituents

Monoterpenes-77%
Sesquiterpenes-12
Alcohols-9%
Esters-7%
Diterpenes-3%

Interesting Fact

The Phoenicians and Cretans used cypress for building ships and bows. Egyptians made coffins of cypress to place inside stone sarcophagi. And the Greeks carved it into statues of their gods. The Greek word "*sempervivens*," from which Cypress' botanical name is derived, means "live forever."

Cypress

When I experience Cypress...

Cypress has been scientifically shown to support the cardiovascular and immune systems.

Frankincense

Daily Uses
Supports a healthy immune system. Supports a healthy respiratory system and normal cell regeneration.

Biblical References
When anyone brings a grain offering to the Lord, their offering is to be of the finest flour. They are to pour olive oil on it, put incense on it

Leviticus 2:1

More References
Exodus 30:34
52 total references!

When I experience Frankincense...

Origins
Frankincense is from the botanical family *Burseraceae* and originates from Somalia and Yemen. Its extraction method is steam distillation from gum/resin.

Key constituents
Monoterpenes-82%
Sesquiterpenes-8%
Alcohols-4%

Interesting Facts
Frankincense is also known as *olibanum*. The word *frankincense* is derived from the Medieval French word for "real incense."

Frankincense is considered the "holy anointing oil" in the Middle East and has been used in religious ceremonies for thousands of years.

Frankincense

When I experience Frankincense...

Frankincense is the second-most mentioned oil of the Bible. It was used for religious rituals, flavoring food and all manner of healing.

Galbanum

Daily Uses
Supports healthy skin, respiratory system and is emotionally balancing. Traditionally used to aid with spiritual grounding and to support meditation.

Biblical References
Then the Lord said to Moses, "Take fragrant spices–gum resin, onycha and galbanum–and pure frankincense, all in equal amounts, and make a fragrant blend of incense, the work of a perfumer. It is to be salted and pure and sacred.

Exodus 30:34-35

When I experience Galbanum...

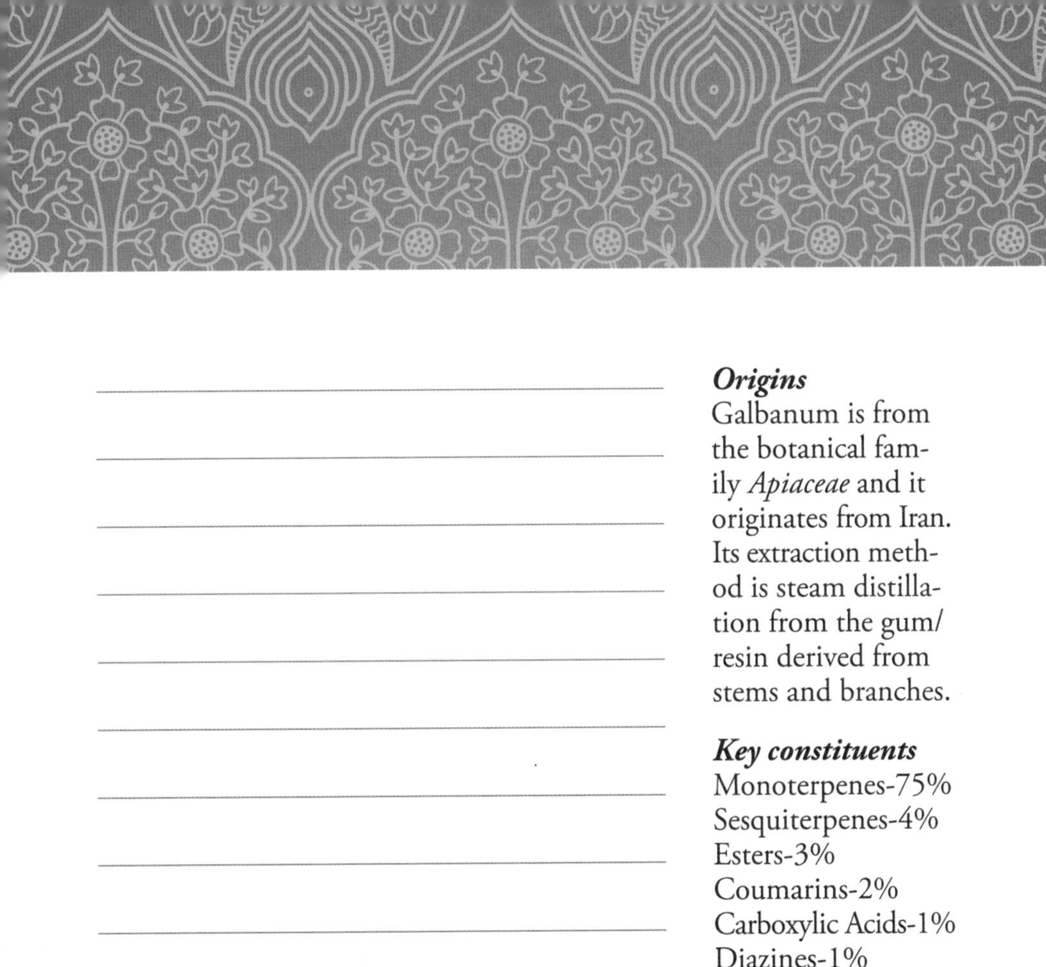

Origins
Galbanum is from the botanical family *Apiaceae* and it originates from Iran. Its extraction method is steam distillation from the gum/resin derived from stems and branches.

Key constituents
Monoterpenes-75%
Sesquiterpenes-4%
Esters-3%
Coumarins-2%
Carboxylic Acids-1%
Diazines-1%
Furanoids 1%

Interesting Fact
Galbanum is mentioned in the Old Testament and in Egyptian medical texts. It is esteemed for its medicinal and spiritual properties.

Galbanum

When I experience Galbanum...

Galbanum was one of the four oils in the holy incense, which has been burned in Jewish temples for millennia.

Hyssop

Daily Uses
Hyssop supports a healthy metabolism and respiratory system. Also comforting to skin.

Biblical References
Take a bunch of hyssop, dip it into the blood in the basin and put some of the blood on the top and on both sides of the door frame. None of you shall go out of the door of your house until morning.
Exodus 12:22

More References
Leviticus 14: 4, 6

When I experience Hyssop...

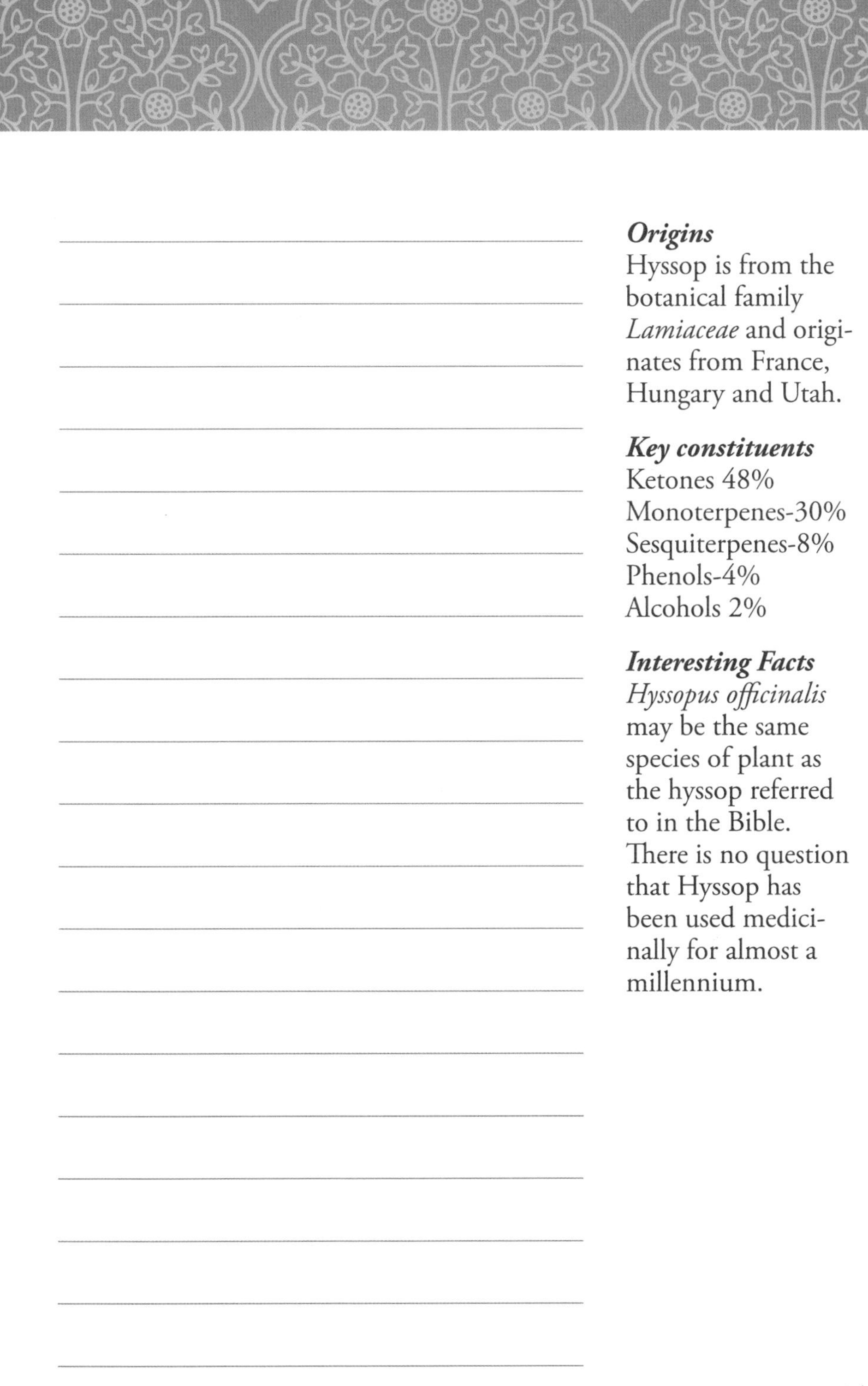

Origins
Hyssop is from the botanical family *Lamiaceae* and originates from France, Hungary and Utah.

Key constituents
Ketones 48%
Monoterpenes-30%
Sesquiterpenes-8%
Phenols-4%
Alcohols 2%

Interesting Facts
Hyssopus officinalis may be the same species of plant as the hyssop referred to in the Bible. There is no question that Hyssop has been used medicinally for almost a millennium.

Hyssop

When I experience Hyssop...

Fragrant herbs such as hyssop were scattered across the floors of Jewish temples where animal sacrifices were offered daily. Their fragrant oils helped to keep the air smelling fresh.

Myrrh

Daily Uses
Supports a healthy immune system. Reduces the look of fine lines, wrinkles and blemishes.

Biblical References
On coming to the house, they saw the child with his mother Mary, and they bowed down and worshipped him. Then they opened their treasures and presented him with gifts of gold, frankincense and myrrh.

Matthew 2:11

More References
Genesis 37:25
Genesis 43:11
Exodus 30:23

When I experience Myrrh...

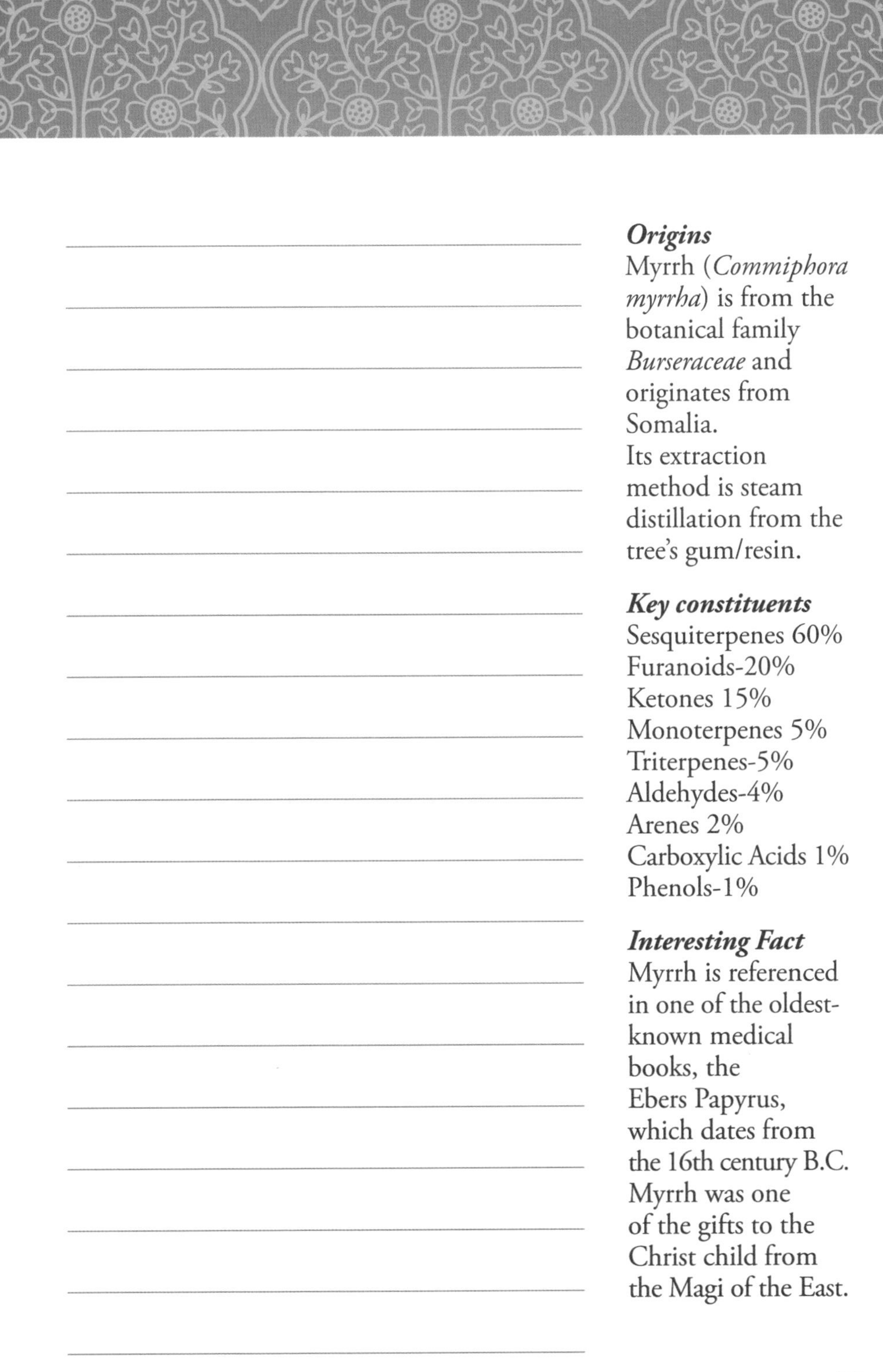

Origins
Myrrh (*Commiphora myrrha*) is from the botanical family *Burseraceae* and originates from Somalia.
Its extraction method is steam distillation from the tree's gum/resin.

Key constituents
Sesquiterpenes 60%
Furanoids-20%
Ketones 15%
Monoterpenes 5%
Triterpenes-5%
Aldehydes-4%
Arenes 2%
Carboxylic Acids 1%
Phenols-1%

Interesting Fact
Myrrh is referenced in one of the oldest-known medical books, the Ebers Papyrus, which dates from the 16th century B.C. Myrrh was one of the gifts to the Christ child from the Magi of the East.

Myrrh

When I experience Myrrh...

The most-mentioned herb in the Bible, myrrh was given to the Christ Child and also offered to Him while on the cross.

Myrtle

Daily Uses
Supports healthy hormone balance and soothes the respiratory system. Promotes circulation for a healthy glow and reduced appearance of fine lines and wrinkles.

Biblical Reference
Instead of the thorn bush will grow the juniper, and instead of briers the myrtle will grow. This will be for the Lord's renown, for an everlasting sign,
that will endure.

Isaiah 55:13

More References
Nehemiah 8:15
Isaiah 41:19

When I experience Myrtle...

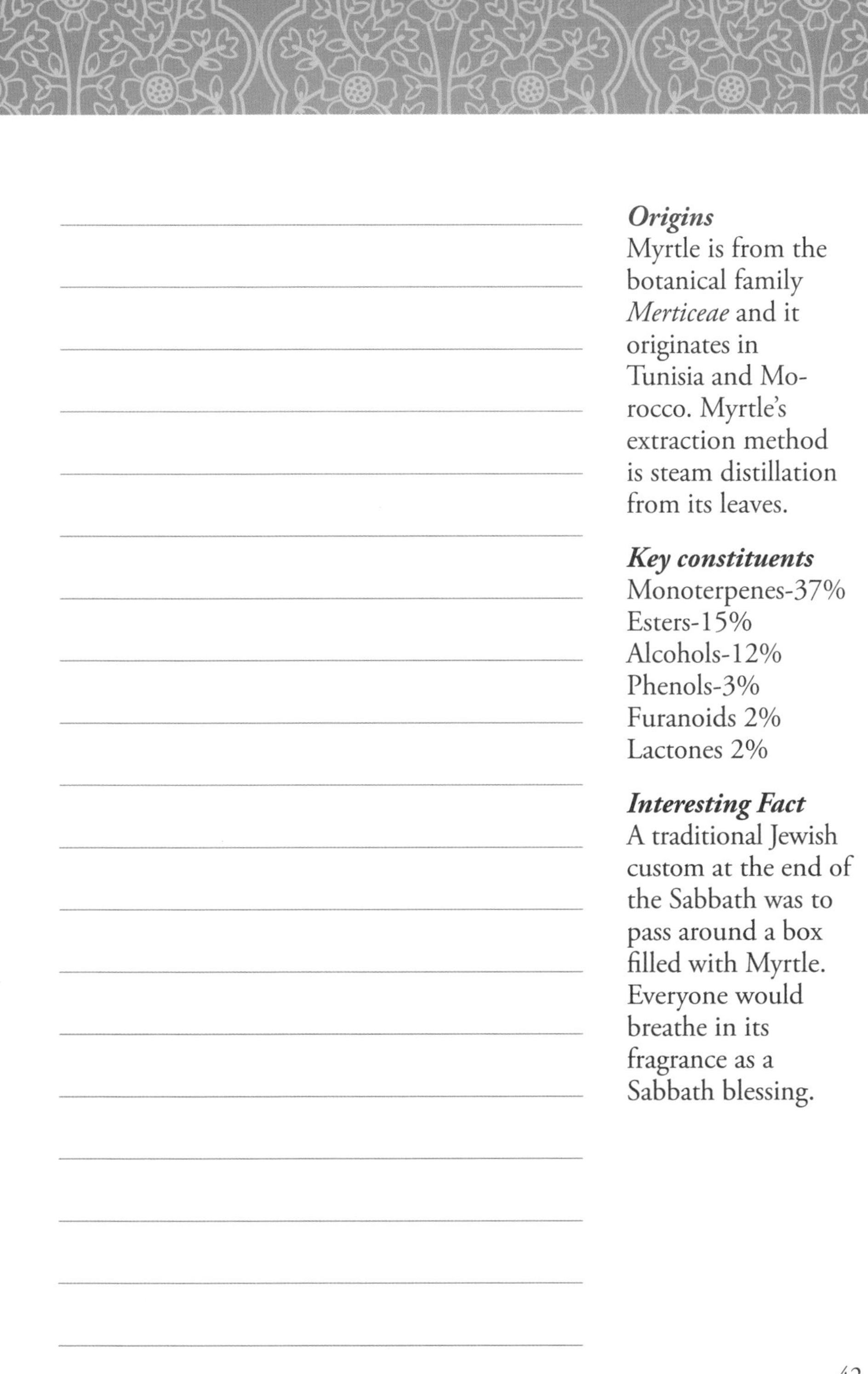

Origins
Myrtle is from the botanical family *Merticeae* and it originates in Tunisia and Morocco. Myrtle's extraction method is steam distillation from its leaves.

Key constituents
Monoterpenes-37%
Esters-15%
Alcohols-12%
Phenols-3%
Furanoids 2%
Lactones 2%

Interesting Fact
A traditional Jewish custom at the end of the Sabbath was to pass around a box filled with Myrtle. Everyone would breathe in its fragrance as a Sabbath blessing.

Myrtle

When I experience Myrtle...

For ancient Jews, the myrtle tree was a symbol of peace and justice, as well as a source for healing oil.

Onycha

Daily Uses
Supports a healthy digestive system and healthy blood sugar levels. Supports a healthy respiratory system. Soothes skin and has a calming effect when used in massage.

Biblical References
Then the Lord said to Moses, "Take fragrant spices–gum resin, onycha and galbanum–and pure frankincense, all in equal amounts, and make a fragrant blend of incense, the work of a perfumer. It is to be salted and pure and sacred.

Exodus 30:34-35

When I experience Onycha...

Origins
Onycha or *Styrax benzoin* is from the botanical family of *Styracaceae*. This essential oil is distilled from the resin of the tree.

Key constituents
Esters-70%
Carboxylic Acids-20%
Aldehydes 2%
Alcohols 1%

Interesting Facts
Onycha is one of the heaviest oils and is too thick to pour. It has a vanilla scent.
Onycha has been used for more than 200 years as "Tincture of Benzoin," an effective hospital antiseptic.

Onycha

When I experience Onycha...

Onycha was used in the holy incense of Exodus 30. Its modern uses are rather extensive.

Rose of Sharon or Cistus

Daily Uses
Supports the immune system and normal cellular regeneration. Promotes relaxation.

Biblical References
I am a rose of Sharon, a lily of the valleys.
Song of Songs 2:1

When I experience Rose of Sharon/Cistus...

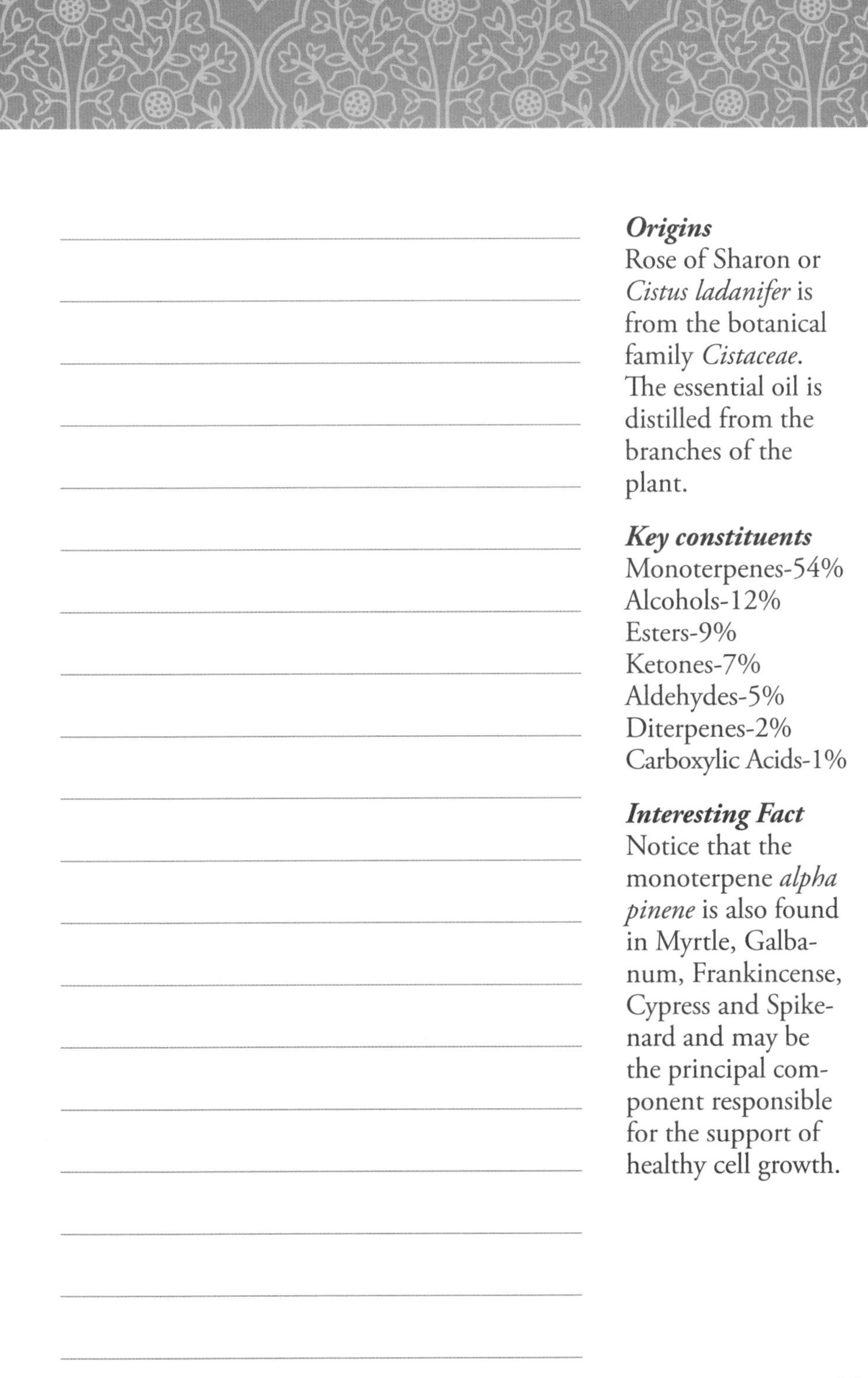

Origins
Rose of Sharon or *Cistus ladanifer* is from the botanical family *Cistaceae*. The essential oil is distilled from the branches of the plant.

Key constituents
Monoterpenes-54%
Alcohols-12%
Esters-9%
Ketones-7%
Aldehydes-5%
Diterpenes-2%
Carboxylic Acids-1%

Interesting Fact
Notice that the monoterpene *alpha pinene* is also found in Myrtle, Galbanum, Frankincense, Cypress and Spikenard and may be the principal component responsible for the support of healthy cell growth.

Rose of Sharon or Cistus

When I experience Rose of Sharon...

Rose of Sharon is a wild bloom that grows on the Plains of Sharon, located west of Jerusalem. This plant has various healing properties.

Spikenard

Daily Uses
Supports healthy cardiovascular and digestive systems. Promotes relaxation and healthy energy levels when diffused.

Biblical References
While the king was at his table, my perfume spread its fragrance.
Song of Songs 1:12

MoreReferences
John 12:1-3
Luke 7:36-38
Mark 14:3
Matthew 26:6-7

When I experience Spikenard...

Origins
Spikenard or *Nardostachys jatamansi* is from the botanical family *Valerianaceae* and originates from India. Its extraction method is steam distillation from the plant's roots.

Key constituents
Sesquiterpenes-50%
Monoterpenes-36%
Phenols-2%
Coumarins-2%
Oxides-2%
Carboxylic Acids-1%

Interesting Facts
Spikenard is highly regarded in India as a medicinal herb. It was one of the most precious oils in ancient times, used only by priests, kings and initiates. The New Testament describes how Mary of Bethany anointed Jesus' feet with spikenard oil before the Last Supper.

Spikenard

When I experience Spikenard...

Ancient Jews used spikenard in the long-esteemed custom of anointing the head and feet of distinguished guests.

Questions & Notes

The first time I tried an essential oil I thought...

Questions & Notes

Describe your experiences with essential oils that convinced you they might actually work.

Questions & Notes

Which essential oils would you like to learn more about? What would you like to learn about each one of them?

Questions & Notes

Have you ever used an oil for one thing and then discovered it supported something else?

Questions & Notes

My favorite diffuser recipes are...

Questions & Notes

When I envision Queen Esther using Myrrh and other beautifying oils, I think of...

Questions & Notes

If I were to really treat myself with a special essential oil, I would buy...

Questions & Notes

Have you ever had an experience where a friend was in need and an oil you gave them worked? If yes, describe the experience.

Questions & Notes

If you could blend an essential oil and have it work according to its name, what would you blend and why?

Questions & Notes

Which emotion would best serve your goals and which oils would support that emotion?

Questions & Notes

When I have a stressful day, I love to use _____ essential oil because it makes me feel _____.

Questions & Notes

My favorite oils to use at bedtime are...

Questions & Notes

When I need to stay focused, I like to diffuse...

Questions & Notes

When I need to get creative, I like to use these oils...

Questions & Notes

If you could give one oil to anyone on the planet and have it work instantly, which oil would you give and to whom?

Questions & Notes

Make your ultimate essential oil wish list.
Which are your top five and why?

Questions & Notes

If you had to choose only one essential oil to use for the rest of your life, which one would you choose and why?

Questions & Notes

Questions & Notes